Where's Ralph?

Sandra Pratt

ISBN 979-8-89243-322-8 (paperback)
ISBN 979-8-89243-323-5 (hardcover)
ISBN 979-8-89243-324-2 (digital)

Copyright © 2024 by Sandra Pratt

All rights reserved. No part of this publication may be reproduced, distributed, or transmitted in any form or by any means, including photocopying, recording, or other electronic or mechanical methods without the prior written permission of the publisher. For permission requests, solicit the publisher via the address below.

Christian Faith Publishing
832 Park Avenue
Meadville, PA 16335
www.christianfaithpublishing.com

Printed in the United States of America

The golden teddy bear hamster was just one of Renee and Ron's Christmas presents. They named their furry little pet Ralph.

Ralph liked his new home. His bright yellow Habitrail was hamster heaven! Ralph scurried around and around on his little red wheel. He crawled up and down the brightly colored transparent tubes. But the curious hamster found the top compartment most interesting. The view from that part of the cage was amazing!

Ralph's shiny black eyes scanned the children's bedroom—the window, the closet, the dresser, the toy chest, and the *door*! Even though Ralph seemed happy in his new home, he was eager to discover what lay beyond the children's bedroom. The day's activities of running and climbing made Ralph tired. So nestling down in the corner of his cage, he fell asleep. His hamster curiosity would just have to wait.

Then night came. The children were sound asleep. But Ralph was wide awake! The busy hamster ran around and around and around on his little red wheel. Faster! Faster! Faster! But no matter how fast Ralph ran, he was still in his cage. After that, Ralph crawled up to the Habitrail's top compartment. But the compartment's lid was tightly closed. So using his head, the determined hamster pushed and nudged until the metal cover fell off. *What better time to explore my new surroundings*, thought Ralph. So placing his tiny paws on the compartment's rim, he jumped down onto the bedroom floor. Now free to discover what lay beyond the children's bedroom, Ralph scampered to the door and wriggled his furry little body under it.

That night, Ralph explored every nook and cranny in his family's apartment. *Wow!* he thought. *This is more fun than running around on my wheel! This is even more exciting than crawling through brightly colored tubes and tunnels!* But as daybreak neared, the adventurous little hamster grew weary. Ralph was fading fast.

Morning came, and the children couldn't wait to play with their new pet. But when they uncovered Ralph's cage, they were surprised to find that…Ralph was gone!

Cries of, "Where's Ralph?" shattered the morning quiet. "Where's Ralph?" "His cage is empty!" Ron called to his mother.

"Oh, where's Ralph?" cried Renee. "The compartment lid is on the floor!"

Mother calmly answered, "He's somewhere in this apartment, children. Just keep looking."

The children looked under the beds and in the beds. They rummaged through their toy chest. They looked under the dresser and in their closet. "Where's Ralph?" the children wondered.

"Ralph is probably sleeping in a dark, quiet place," said Mother. "Hamsters are nocturnal creatures. They sleep during the day and scurry about at night."

So the search for the missing hamster continued from one room to another.

The children peered under the sofa and chairs in the living room. No Ralph.

Renee ran to the dining area and looked behind the china closet. No Ralph.

Ron dashed to the kitchen and checked behind the trash can. He even peeked under the stove. Still no Ralph.

"Oh, where's Ralph? They cried.

"Not to worry, children," Mother calmly answered. "There *is* one place we haven't looked."

Then Mother slowly and quietly opened the door to the storage closet. One by one, she removed the broom, the mop, and the vacuum cleaner. And all the way in the back of the closet, resting on a small bed of hamster fluff mixed with newspaper bits, lay Ralph—sound asleep! *That curious hamster must have made several trips from his cage to the closet during the night*, she thought.

"Children," whispered Mother, "the search is over. Here's Ralph!" Gently scooping him up in her hands, she carried the sleeping hamster back to his cage. The children were happy. Mother was happy. Ralph looked happy too! Perhaps he was dreaming of his all-night adventure in his new home.

About the Author

SANDRA PRATT

Sandra Pratt lives in Mount Laurel, New Jersey. She is a retired elementary school teacher and a graduate of Temple University, Philadelphia, Pennsylvania. After thirty years in the classroom, Sandra continued using her teaching gifts by tutoring adults in the English language, as well as mentoring elementary school students.

Sandra has served as a Sunday school teacher, superintendent, and Vacation Bible School director. She has also developed several VBS programs. Her favorite program is "In Search of the Son—Before Bethlehem and Beyond!" Sandra currently assists in Sunday school, sings with the worship team, and is studying classical Hebrew.

Sandra has been writing poetry and children's stories in rhyme for over forty years. This delightful story, *Where's Ralph?*, was inspired by an amusing event that occurred many years ago. Sandra lives in close proximity to five of her six grandchildren and enjoys spending time with them.